# The Church Must Send or It Will End

**DAG HEWARD-MILLS**

*Parchment House*

Unless otherwise stated, all Scripture quotations are taken from the King James Version of the Bible.

THE CHURCH MUST SEND OR IT WILL END

Copyright © 2022 Dag Heward-Mills

First published by Parchment House 2022

Published by Parchment House 2022
1st Printing 2022

Find out more about Dag Heward-Mills at:
Healing Jesus Campaign
Write to: evangelist@daghewardmills.org
Website: www.daghewardmills.org
Facebook: Dag Heward-Mills
Twitter: @EvangelistDag

ISBN: 978-1-64330-519-6

All rights reserved under international copyright law. Written permission must be secured from the publisher to use or reproduce any part of this book.

## *Contents*

1. What Causes the End to Come? .......................................... 1
2. The End of Lucifer's Ministry ............................................ 4
3. The End of Adam's Ministry ............................................. 10
4. The End of Cain's Ministry ............................................... 14
5. The End of the Men of Sodom ......................................... 18
6. The End of Eli's Ministry ................................................. 22
7. The End of Saul's Ministry ............................................... 25
8. The End of Absalom's Ministry ........................................ 29
9. The End of Gehazi's Ministry .......................................... 34
10. The End of Vashti ............................................................ 38
11. The End of a Congregation .............................................. 41
12. The End of Judas' Ministry .............................................. 46
13. The End of the Church's Ministry ................................... 50
14. The End of Babylon ......................................................... 54
15. The End of the World ...................................................... 58
16. The End of John the Baptist's Ministry .......................... 61
17. The End of Onan's Ministry ............................................ 65
18. The End of Isaac's Ministry ............................................. 69
19. The End of Ahab .............................................................. 72
20. The End of Ministry ........................................................ 76

# CHAPTER 1

# What Causes the End to Come?

But the end of all things is at hand: be ye therefore sober, and watch unto prayer.

1 Peter 4:7

The end of a life is always precipitated by something. This book seeks to find out what causes the "end" to happen. What will end your life? What will end your ministry?

What can end life as you know it? Is there anything that has the power to precipitate the end of all things in your life?

How does the end come? What makes things come to an end?

The end of everything is death! There are many causes of death. There are also many things that have ended the ministries of God's servants. In this book, you will see what ended the ministries of God's great servants. Through this revelation, your ministry will be delivered from ending in the same unfortunate way.

**... and then shall the end come.**
**Matthew 24:14**

Death and accidents are never taken lightly anywhere in the world because they signify the end of life. When a plane crashes, great efforts are made to find out why the plane crashed. When a flight from Rio de Janeiro to Paris crashed in the deepest part of the seas, unmanned nuclear submarines were deployed to locate the little black box of the plane. The airline desperately wanted to know why a perfectly normal jet would disappear in mid-air and plunge into the ocean. Indeed, the same thing could happen again, affecting even more people.

You must learn from anything that has been brought to an end. You must study the endings of ministries. You must analyse the endings of people's lives.

You must learn also from anyone who has been brought to an unfortunate end. Whatever has happened to someone can happen to you. Many things happen for our admonition.

Now all these things happened unto them for ensamples: and they are written for our admonition, upon whom the ends of the world are come.

1 Corinthians 10:11

Many of the characters in this book came to an unfortunate end. It is important to know why their lives ended. It is important to know why people's ministries come to an end. What is it that triggers the end? What will trigger the end for you? What will be the sign of the end of your ministry on this earth?

What will bring an end to the church? What will bring the end to your church? There are many churches that I know of which have come to an end. They do not exist any longer. Our church has bought buildings that belonged to other churches that came to an end. What is it that will end your church's lifecycle? A famous man of God once said, "The church must send or it will end!" This is a true saying and we must examine it so that we receive the wisdom from this mysterious statement.

# CHAPTER 2

# The End of Lucifer's Ministry

> Thou art the anointed cherub that covereth; and I have set thee so: thou wast upon the holy mountain of God; thou hast walked up and down in the midst of the stones of fire.
>
> **Ezekiel 28:14**

*The End of Lucifer's Ministry*

Lucifer was anointed. Lucifer knows more about the anointing than you probably do. Lucifer was the anointed cherub. He lived and worked on the holy mountain of God. Lucifer's work included walking up and down before the presence of God in the midst of stones of fire. Lucifer's ministry came to an unfortunate end. Lucifer was brought down from his high and lofty ministry. This unfortunate demise and demotion is what satan wishes for everyone he attacks. He wants everyone to fall and to be destroyed just as he was destroyed.

Lucifer fell before our world began. Lucifer means "the shining one." He was the morning star, unique and radiant. Lucifer was the most gifted, most outstanding of all the angels. It is only after Lucifer fell that he was changed into what we now know as satan, the dragon. Satan simply means the "opposer." Lucifer has changed from a bright, shining, attractive angel into an ugly opposer and adversary.

**Thou wast perfect in thy ways from the day that thou wast created, till iniquity was found in thee.**
**Ezekiel 28:15**

The reign of Lucifer, as he was known, came to an end. What contributed to his destruction? Pride brought the life and ministry of Lucifer to an abrupt and tragic end.

Your ministry will come to an end because of your pride.

Thy pomp is brought down to the grave, and the noise of thy viols: the worm is spread under thee, and the worms cover thee. How art thou fallen from heaven, O Lucifer, son of the morning! how art thou cut down to the ground, which didst weaken the nations!

For thou hast said in thine heart, I WILL ASCEND into heaven, I WILL EXALT my throne above the stars of God: I WILL SIT ALSO upon the mount of the congregation, in the sides of the north: I WILL ASCEND above the heights of the clouds; I WILL BE LIKE the most High.

Isaiah 14:11-14

The original sin of Lucifer was pride and selfish ambition. Lucifer was lifted up in pride. He said, "I will" five times. Each time he said, "I will" he was exalting himself in pride. His pride led to his destruction. God responded to Lucifer's proudly spoken "I will" statements. Almighty God released five "I will" statements to counteract each of Lucifer's proud "I wills."

> Thou wast perfect in thy ways from the day that thou wast created, till iniquity was found in thee. By the multitude of thy merchandise they have filled the midst of thee with violence, and thou hast sinned: therefore I WILL CAST THEE AS PROFANE out of the mountain of God: and I WILL DESTROY THEE, O covering cherub, from the midst of the stones of fire. Thine heart was lifted up because of thy beauty, thou hast corrupted thy wisdom by reason of thy brightness: I WILL CAST THEE TO THE GROUND, I WILL LAY THEE BEFORE KINGS, that they may behold thee. Thou hast defiled thy sanctuaries by the multitude of thine iniquities, by the iniquity of thy traffick; therefore WILL I BRING FORTH A FIRE FROM THE MIDST OF THEE, it shall devour thee, and I WILL BRING THEE TO ASHES upon the earth in the sight of all them that behold thee.
>
> Ezekiel 28:15-18

When God spoke those statements, Lucifer's reign as the shining one came to an end. He was cast to the ground and became nothing. This was the end of Lucifer! Lucifer's end came because of pride. Your end can also come because of pride. The church can also end because of pride. Pride does not just come before a fall. Pride comes before your destruction.

I have appointed thousands of pastors into the ministry. I have also had the unfortunate experience of dealing with difficulties, sin and rebellion. I can surely say every single one of these difficult cases involved pride. You may think that a person just has a problem with immorality. However, you will always find the element of pride somewhere. Usually, immoral people become proud in their sin and this gives them a false confidence to carry on going further and further into sin. It is this pride that often leads them to be discovered, unravelled and uncovered.

Rebellious and disloyal men are often proud. It is their pride that gives them the confidence to attack authorities. It is pride that enables people to attack their fathers and speak to them as equals.

When people are proud, they set aside ancient scriptures and re-evaluate teachings they themselves have taught. They will say things like; "Honour your father does not mean you should be blind to your father's obvious errors". Proud people begin to say things like, "Touch not the Lord's anointed is a scripture that is being misused and misunderstood by authority figures who are doing wrong things."

Pride was the end of Lucifer and pride is usually the end of many in the ministry.

Pride is like a virus which has many presentations. A viral disease can present as weakness, fever, loss of smell, pain, depression, general malaise, severe life-threatening symptoms, headaches, nausea, vomiting, dizziness and so on. Indeed, you can hardly tell what sickness you are suffering from when you experience a viral illness.

Pride is like that! It has so many presentations. A proud person may manifest by laughing at someone. A proud person may manifest by talking about someone, criticizing someone. Pride may manifest itself in the topic you choose to preach about or write about. Plain confidence may even be a manifestation of pride. Over confidence may be a more obvious manifestation of pride. Quarrelling and contention are signs of pride. Only pride makes you have certain quarrels. The Bible describes this.

**Only by pride cometh contention: but with the well advised is wisdom.**

**Proverbs 13:10**

It is important to pray for the Spirit of humility so that you are enveloped in a cloak of humility. Pride is waiting at the door to end your ministry. The end will come when pride takes over. Fight to be a humble person. The greatest gift you can have is the gift of humility, lowliness and meekness. These character traits are easier listed than achieved. It is easy to say "I want to be humble" but it is not easy to be humble. It is not easy to be humble because it is not easy to know when you are not being humble.

God will give you many experiences that will force you to be humble. Most of these experiences are the painful disappointments of life. In the ministry, you can sit down in disillusionment, discouragement and disbelief, wondering how you got yourself into certain situations and how you will ever climb back into a higher level. God has a plan for you. God will fight for you and help you when you genuinely call on Him.

Mary the mother of Jesus was chosen to do the greatest job a woman could ever ask for. She was to bear the Son of God. She was to carry the holy seed and present the Saviour to the world. Why was she blessed among women? Was it because of her singing gift? Was it because of her beauty? Was it because of her preaching ability? I do not think so! It was because of her humility.

There is only one passage that records the words of the Holy Virgin Mary. In this passage, she uses words which give us a revelation of whom she was.

She says; You have regarded my *low estate*! You have lifted up someone who is of a *low degree*!

These two descriptions, low degree and low estate, reveal the humility and lowliness of Mary. No wonder she was chosen. Humility is the beginning of wisdom when you are relating with God. Pride is the end of the relationship with God.

And Mary said, My soul doth magnify the Lord, And my spirit hath rejoiced in God my Saviour. FOR HE HATH REGARDED THE LOW ESTATE OF HIS HANDMAIDEN: for, behold, from henceforth all generations shall call me blessed. For he that is mighty hath done to me great things; and holy is his name. And his mercy is on them that fear him from generation to generation. He hath shewed strength with his arm; he hath scattered the proud in the imagination of their hearts. HE HATH PUT DOWN THE MIGHTY FROM THEIR SEATS, AND EXALTED THEM OF LOW DEGREE.

Luke 1:46-52

# CHAPTER 3

# The End of Adam's Ministry

Therefore the Lord God sent him forth from the garden of Eden, to till the ground from whence he was taken. SO HE DROVE OUT THE MAN; and he placed at the east of the garden of Eden Cherubims, and a flaming sword which turned every way, to keep the way of the tree of life.

**Genesis 3:23-24**

*The End of Adam's Ministry*

Adam, the first man, was put in charge of this glorious world. He ruled from Alaska to Cape Town. His domain was the whole world. Unfortunately, his reign was cut short. Why was that? Why did Adam change from being the father of a super race into the father of a beggarly sinful race? How come Adam is the father of billions of suffering, sick, wicked, lost and depraved human beings? Let us look at why Adam's life and ministry ended.

## Your Ministry Will Come to an End because of Another Voice

> Now the serpent was more subtil than any beast of the field which the Lord God had made. And he said unto the woman, Yea, hath God said, ye shall not eat of every tree of the garden? And the woman said unto the serpent, We may eat of the fruit of the trees of the garden: But of the fruit of the tree which is in the midst of the garden, God hath said, Ye shall not eat of it, neither shall ye touch it, lest ye die. And the serpent said unto the woman, Ye shall not surely die: For God doth know that in the day ye eat thereof, then your eyes shall be opened, and ye shall be as gods, knowing good and evil. And when the woman saw that the tree was good for food, and that it was pleasant to the eyes, and a tree to be desired to make one wise, she took of the fruit thereof, and did eat, and gave also unto her husband with her; and he did eat.
>
> And the eyes of them both were opened, and they knew that they were naked; and they sewed fig leaves together, and made themselves aprons. And they heard the voice of the Lord God walking in the garden in the cool of the day: and Adam and his wife hid themselves from the presence of the Lord God amongst the trees of the garden. And the Lord God called unto Adam, and said unto him, Where art thou? And he said, I heard thy voice in the garden, and I was afraid, because I was naked; and I hid myself.
>
> Genesis 3:1-10

## Your Ministry Will End if You Follow the Voice of the Devil instead of the Voice of God

Adam brought destruction to the entire human race by listening to another voice. His wife, who was one with him, listened to the devil. By opening herself up to the voice of the devil, she disconnected from God. You cannot listen to two voices at the same time.

Jesus Christ was the second Adam. The first Adam failed to reject a third voice. Jesus did not fall for that trick. When satan tempted Adam in the garden, he fell headlong into the trap. When Jesus encountered the devil in the wilderness, He simply would not countenance any suggestion that came from the devil. There are things the devil suggested to Jesus that were not outright evil. For instance, turning stones into bread is not a sin. But once the idea did not come from God, Jesus did not want to have anything to do with it.

Whose voice are you listening to? Who advises you? You either listen to the voice of God or you listen to the voice of the devil. The voice you listen to will determine your future. All the good things in your life will come to an end because you listened to another voice which you are not supposed to listen to.

## Your Ministry Will End if You Follow the Voice of Your Wife instead of Following the Voice of God

> And unto Adam he said, BECAUSE THOU HAST HEARKENED UNTO THE VOICE OF THY WIFE, and hast eaten of the tree, of which I commanded thee, saying, Thou shalt not eat of it: cursed is the ground for thy sake; in sorrow shalt thou eat of it all the days of thy life;
>
> Genesis 3:17

Adam's life and ministry ended because he listened to the voice of his wife. Adam listened to his wife. He should have listened to God instead. It is not easy to ignore what your wife says. The Bible says husbands should love their wives. Most husbands interpret that loving their wives means they must listen to their wives and obey them. If Jesus had listened to a wife He would not have died on a cross for us. If Abraham had listened to his wife, he would not have been ready to sacrifice his son Isaac to the Lord. If you do get married, it is important to remain fiercely loyal to God.

One of the subtle but major tests of ministry is to discern when a voice you are listening to is contrary to the voice of God. Jesus was close to Peter. Peter became familiar with Jesus. Peter crossed the line when he sought to prevent Jesus from dying on the cross. Jesus gave Peter one of the most debilitating rebukes of all time by calling him "satan". Jesus refused to listen to any other voice. He especially chose to rebuke the voice of His beloved Peter, whom He had just appointed as the head of the church. If you become a man of great authority, you should expect this particular test; the test of the third voice.

## Your Ministry Will End if You Follow a Third Voice

In your relationships you must ensure that you do not have a third voice. If your pastor is relating with you and there is a third party speaking to you, you will be affected by the third party. You will never be the same as someone who does not have a third party influencing them from behind the scenes. Even your marriage will be negatively affected if you have the voice of a third party.

# CHAPTER 4

# The End of Cain's Ministry

And in process of time it came to pass, that Cain brought of the fruit of the ground an offering unto the Lord.

And Abel, he also brought of the firstlings of his flock and of the fat thereof. And the Lord had respect unto Abel and to his offering: BUT UNTO CAIN AND TO HIS OFFERING HE HAD NOT RESPECT. And Cain was very wroth, and his countenance fell....
And now art thou cursed from the earth, which hath opened her mouth to receive thy brother's blood from thy hand; When thou tillest the ground, it shall not henceforth yield unto thee her strength; a fugitive and a vagabond shalt thou be in the earth.

Genesis 4:3-5, 11-12

## 1. Your ministry will be brought to an end when God does not respect your offerings.

**And in process of time it came to pass, that Cain brought of the fruit of the ground an offering unto the Lord. And Abel, he also brought of the firstlings of his flock and of the fat thereof. And the Lord had respect unto Abel and to his offering:**

**Genesis 4:3-4**

Cain was one of only two ministers on the earth. He had great opportunities ahead of him. His special position was taken away and he became a vagabond. What brought about the destruction of Cain's ministry?

Cain's life and ministry came to an end when his offering was rejected. Cain offered God some vegetables instead of offering Him a blood sacrifice. Cain's life and ministry were brought to an end because his offering was not respected by God. Do not allow your life and ministry to come to an end.

God does not respect offerings that are meaningless. He wants a blood sacrifice. Many people want to present their own ideas to God and live according to them. But God will have His way! You cannot offer God two hours on Sunday evening when He actually wants your whole life. You cannot tell God to be satisfied with two hours every Tuesday when He actually wants your whole life. You cannot tell God to be satisfied with your old age when He wants your youthful days.

Ministry is about giving everything to God. When you come to God He expects a blood sacrifice. You must give Him your life. You must give Him everything. Cain came along with some vegetables and some salad leaves. There are some people who do not like salad. God did not appreciate, like or want the salad leaves that Cain had brought. God has His standards.

When God does not respect your offering, your whole life will be in jeopardy. There will be no power in your finances. There will be no power to sustain you. There will be no power to make you flourish. You cannot steal from God and expect to prosper.

Give God a real offering of love and of sacrifice. Give Him your time. Give Him your days! Give Him your energy! Give Him your heart! God will have respect on your offering.

2. **Your ministry will come to an end when you attack your brothers.**

   **And Cain talked with Abel his brother: and it came to pass, when they were in the field, that CAIN ROSE UP AGAINST ABEL HIS BROTHER, AND SLEW HIM. And the Lord said unto Cain, Where is Abel thy brother? And he said, I know not: Am I my brother's keeper? And he said, what hast thou done? The voice of thy brother's blood crieth unto me from the ground. And now art thou cursed from the earth, which hath opened her mouth to receive thy brother's blood from thy hand; When thou tillest the ground, it shall not henceforth yield unto thee her strength; a fugitive and a vagabond shalt thou be in the earth.**
   **Genesis 4:8-12**

Cain received a withering curse when he attacked his own brother and killed him. Many pastors attack their fellow pastors. Instead of concentrating on their work, pastors sit down and discuss other ministries, other pastors and other churches. Pastors attack and criticize one another instead of concentrating on the work of ministry that lies undone.

Let us concentrate on the Great Commission and on how to go to the ends of the earth, so that we can all join in the harvest of souls.

It is time to leave other ministers to God. If someone is doing something wrong, leave him to God. God's judgment is greater than your criticism of him. Do not attack your brother. Your ministry can come to an end because of your attack on another person's ministry.

One day, I observed a minister attacking another ministry. I wondered to myself as I watched what this fellow did. A church had been involved in a scandal and the pastor had been caught up in adultery. A group of church members from this church which had the moral problem had moved over to another church.

When the senior pastor of this other church noticed these new comers, he shouted out from the pulpit, "You guys who are coming from so-and-so's church, stand up." He made them all stand up on Sunday morning and told them publicly that they were contaminated Christians because their pastor had been involved in adultery and fornication. He informed them that he was going to cleanse them of the contamination and defilement they had received by belonging to that other church. These church members then humbly received the announcements and the cleansing.

Dear friend, it is only with the passage of time that you discover that the word of God is never broken. As the years went by I noticed how this particular "cleansing pastor" went from scandal to scandal and from failure to failure. The end of your ministry usually comes when you attack your brother. This pastor who took it upon himself to cleanse his new members publicly ended up in exactly the same difficulty. He was driven out of the pulpit by angry associates who accused him of being immoral. As his immorality and sin increased, his wife also abandoned him. His end was pitiful as is the end of all those who attack their brothers!

# CHAPTER 5

# The End of the Men of Sodom

But the men of Sodom were wicked and sinners before the Lord exceedingly.
Genesis 13:13

And the Lord said, Because the cry of Sodom and Gomorrah is great, and because their sin is very grievous; I will go down now, and see whether they have done altogether according to the cry of it, which is come unto me; and if not, I will know.
Genesis 18:20-21

Then the Lord rained upon Sodom and upon Gomorrah brimstone and fire from the Lord out of heaven; And he overthrew those cities, and all the plain, and all the inhabitants of the cities, and that which grew upon the ground.
Genesis 19:24-25

Even as Sodom and Gomorrah, and the cities about them in like manner, giving themselves over to fornication, and going after strange flesh, are set forth for an example, suffering the vengeance of eternal fire.
Jude 1:7

## Sexual Perversion Will End Your Ministry

Sexual perversion will bring an end to your church. God does not approve of people having sex with animals. God does not approve of sexual perverts. Read it for yourself in different versions of the Bible. Today, there are churches that accept this practice, even in the priesthood. Many of these churches are dead or dying. Many churches which accept this practice have hundreds of empty buildings with no one to attend church in them.

The life in the church is gone because human beings have gone astray from the word of God. God's attitude towards sexual perversion is forever revealed in the Bible. Never forget that sexual perversion brought an end to entire cities. Sexual perversion will bring an end to many churches and denominations turning them into relics and museums that only reveal their past glory. All through the Old Testament and the New Testament, these things are considered as abhorrent practices. Notice the scripture:

> **"Do not practice homosexuality, having sex with another man as with a woman. It is a detestable sin." A man must not defile himself by having sex with an animal. And a woman must not offer herself to a male animal to have intercourse with it. This is a perverse act.**
>
> **Leviticus 18:22-23 (NLT)**

> **Thou shalt not lie with mankind, as with womankind: it is abomination. Neither shalt thou lie with any beast to defile thyself therewith: neither shall any woman stand before a beast to lie down thereto: it is confusion.**
>
> **Leviticus 18:22-23**

> **Do not have sexual relations with a man as one does with a woman; that is detestable.**

**Do not have sexual relations with an animal and defile yourself with it. A woman must not present herself to an animal to have sexual relations with it; that is a perversion.**

**Leviticus 18:22-23 (NIV)**

Sexual perversion is a grievous sin before the Lord. No matter what any government says about sexual perversion, the Bible rejects it. None of us is qualified to edit the Bible and delete certain verses. The Bible is not a Chemistry book that is subject to human revisions every few years. All of us who practice these things must be careful of God's judgment. Sodom and Gomorrah stand as a pattern of what will happen to those who give themselves to sexual perversion. Many modern nations are setting themselves up to become modern Sodom and Gomorrah cities.

Widespread, arrogant and blatant sexual perversion often precede the judgments of God. This wicked world can expect the divine judgment of fire and brimstone as it marches on in the same sins that wiped out the ancient cities of Sodom and Gomorrah. The Bible is the guide for all that we do and all that we believe.

Just as lying, stealing, fornication, adultery and murder are considered sins in the Bible, sexual perversion is equally considered as a sin. If freedom of religion is allowed, then Christianity must be allowed to express all the virtues and beliefs of its religion. If it is a human right to choose to believe and practice your religion, then the religion called Christianity, which is based on the Bible, considers sexual perversion as one of its grievous sins along with other sins like lying, stealing, fornication, adultery and murder. Notice how Paul lists sexual perverts along with other grievous sins. "Or do you not know that wrongdoers will not inherit the kingdom of God? Do not be deceived: Neither the sexually immoral nor idolaters nor adulterers nor men who have sex with men nor thieves nor the greedy nor drunkards nor slanderers nor swindlers will inherit the kingdom of God" (1 Corinthians 6:9-10, NIV). In the New Testament, several passages warn us about practicing sexual perversion.

> **Don't you realize that those who do wrong will not inherit the Kingdom of God? Don't fool yourselves. Those who indulge in sexual sin, or who worship idols, or commit adultery, or are male prostitutes, OR practice homosexuality, or are thieves, or greedy people, or drunkards, or are abusive, or cheat people— none of these will inherit the Kingdom of God.**
>
> **1 Corinthians 6:9-10 (NLT)**

> **For the law was not intended for people who do what is right. It is for people who are lawless and rebellious, who are ungodly and sinful, who consider nothing sacred and defile what is holy, who kill their father or mother or commit other murders.**
>
> **The law is for people who are sexually immoral, or who practice homosexuality, or are slave traders, liars, promise breakers, or who do anything else that contradicts the wholesome teaching**
>
> **1 Timothy 1:9-10 (NLT)**

> **And don't forget Sodom and Gomorrah and their neighboring towns, which were filled with immorality and every kind of sexual perversion. Those cities were destroyed by fire and serve as a warning of the eternal fire of God's judgment.**
>
> **Jude 1:7 (NLT)**

# CHAPTER 6

# The End of Eli's Ministry

Wherefore kick ye at my sacrifice and at mine offering, which I have commanded in my habitation; and honourest thy sons above me, to make yourselves fat with the chiefest of all the offerings of Israel my people? Wherefore the Lord God of Israel saith, I said indeed that thy house, and the house of thy father, should walk before me for ever: BUT NOW THE LORD SAITH, BE IT FAR FROM ME; FOR THEM THAT HONOUR ME I WILL HONOUR, AND THEY THAT DESPISE ME SHALL BE LIGHTLY ESTEEMED.
Behold, the days come, that I will cut off thine arm, and the arm of thy father's house, that there shall not be an old man in thine house. And thou shalt see an enemy in my habitation, in all the wealth which God shall give Israel: and there shall not be an old man in thine house for ever. And the man of thine, whom I shall not cut off from mine altar, shall be to consume thine eyes, and to grieve thine heart: and all the increase of thine house shall die in the flower of their age. And this shall be a sign unto thee, that shall come upon thy two sons, on Hophni and Phinehas; in one day they shall die both of them.

1 Samuel 2:29-34

# Honouring Your Family above the Lord Will End Your Ministry

Eli's priesthood ended abruptly because he honoured his sons above the honour that he gave to God. It is good to handle your family well. It is good to love your family and care for them zealously.

However, Eli's ministry came to an end when he respected his sons more than he respected the commandments of God. Today, many ministries are dwindling because the founders handed them over to their biological children who run them to the ground. Many biological children do not have the call of God.

For many people, it is so important that their biological children own the ministry and have the financial benefits thereof. However, it is important to honour God more than you honour your own biological family. God loves to be respected. God is higher than your biological family.

Eli and his family received a withering curse. Perhaps this is the most debilitating curse in the whole Bible. If you read the details of the curse, you will be left wondering why such a severe punishment was meted out to Eli. It should warn you that an end can come if you raise your family above God.

Today, many people have more respect for their wives and children than they do for God and His work. Anything that takes them away from their family is rejected outright. Yet, people are ready to do jobs that take them away from their families for many years. There are people who travel around for months on end. They are spies and secret service agents for their countries. They live double lives and sacrifice their families for their nations.

When God calls some people to serve Him and to take up their crosses, most of the church rejects the call. Some parents refuse to allow their children to become missionaries and actively discourage them from giving their lives to the service of the King.

Churches which have given themselves wholly to promote happy marriages, family life and the bringing up of children in such a way that it kills the work of God, should be careful that they do not cross a certain line. We must not cross the line that Eli crossed when he honoured his children and his family above God.

> ... But now the Lord saith, Be it far from me; for them that honour me I will honour, and they that despise me shall be lightly esteemed.
>
> 1 Samuel 2:30

# CHAPTER 7

# The End of Saul's Ministry

And Samuel said, Hath the Lord as great delight in burnt offerings and sacrifices, as in obeying the voice of the Lord? Behold, to obey is better than sacrifice, and to hearken than the fat of rams.
For rebellion is as the sin of witchcraft, and stubbornness is as iniquity and idolatry. Because thou hast rejected the word of the Lord, he hath also rejected thee from being king.

                                        1 Samuel 15:22-23

# Stubbornness and Rebellion Will End Your Ministry

Rebellion is connected to demonic activity. Witchcraft has to do with illegitimate and demonic power. Illegitimate and unauthorised power is demonic power. It is an alternative power other than the power of God. Stubbornness always reveals the presence of devils. The presence of devils always reveals that you are near the end.

Stubbornness is connected to demonic activity. Stubbornness has to do with iniquity and idol worship. Idols are demon gods. Idols are inventions of devils. Most idols depict what a demon looks like. The devil is the one who tempted Jesus to worship him instead of God. All idol worship is therefore directly connected to satan. Stubbornness is connected to iniquity and idolatry as well as to satan and demonic activity. Satanic activity always reveals a nearness to the end.

God was upset with Saul for not wiping out the Amalekites. Saul argued with Samuel even though Saul was in the wrong. Stubbornness and disobedience were the hallmarks of Saul's reign as king. These two characteristics brought an end to the ministry of Saul (1 Samuel 15:1-26).

Let there be no stubbornness in your life. It can bring about the end of your ministry. Be quick to agree! Be quick to see! Be quick to flow! Be quick to take corrections! Otherwise, the end will come prematurely.

Stubbornness is such a serious problem that stubborn children were put to death, according to the Law of Moses.

> IF A MAN HAVE A STUBBORN AND REBELLIOUS SON, which will not obey the voice of his father, or the voice of his mother, and that, when they have chastened him, will not hearken unto them: Then shall his father and his mother lay hold on him, and bring him out unto the elders of his city, and unto the gate of his place; And

they shall say unto the elders of his city, This our son is stubborn and rebellious, he will not obey our voice; he is a glutton, and a drunkard. And ALL THE MEN OF HIS CITY SHALL STONE HIM WITH STONES, THAT HE DIE: so shalt thou put evil away from among you; and all Israel shall hear, and fear.

Deuteronomy 21:18-21

This harsh response to stubbornness by the Law of Moses reveals the seriousness of the sin of stubbornness. It reveals how stubbornness is connected to demonic activity. Beware of developing a mind that never changes.

I remember counselling two young pastors. Both of them had the same contentious problem in relation to their senior pastor. I gave both of them the same advice.

I told them, "Only by pride cometh contention. Back down from this conflict and do not try to prove that you are right. Leave it to God. Promotion does not come from the east or from the west. God is the One who will promote you in the ministry."

One of the pastors believed and obeyed. He ended up well and continued with his ministry. The other pastor stubbornly continued in his error. No one, including myself, was able to change his course or counsel him. He ended up as a beggar! Stubbornness is a revelation of the number of demons that are in you. Stubbornness is a revelation that the demonic influence in your life is very strong. Of course, when demons are part of your ministry you can only expect the end to be near.

Rebellion is a highly demonic manifestation. Rebellion always involves rising up against authority. Rebellion involves rising up against any form of control. Rebellion involves rising up against established tradition. People who give themselves to defying and resisting spiritual authorities are rebellious.

Rebellion is seen when there is an issue that involves correction. Rebellion is revealed when somebody has to be instructed, directed or reproved. The reaction to correction is always a revelation of whom you are dealing with.

**Reprove not a scorner, lest he hate thee: rebuke a wise man, and he will love thee.**

**Proverbs 9:8**

As people stay longer in the ministry, they become harder and harder to correct. Their long stay in the ministry hardens them and makes them proud. They begin to have proud and stubborn reactions to correction. These negative reactions can lead to the end of their ministry.

# CHAPTER 8

# The End of Absalom's Ministry

And Absalom met the servants of David. And Absalom rode upon a mule, and the mule went under the thick boughs of a great oak, and his head caught hold of the oak, and he was taken up between the heaven and the earth; and the mule that was under him went away. And a certain man saw it, and told Joab, and said, Behold, I saw Absalom hanged in an oak.... Then said Joab, I may not tarry thus with thee. And he took three darts in his hand, and thrust them through the heart of Absalom, while he was yet alive in the midst of the oak. And ten young men that bare Joab's armour compassed about and smote Absalom, and slew him.

2 Samuel 18:9-10, 14-15

# Attacking Your Father Will End Your Ministry

Absalom stands out as the person who attacked his own father. Honouring your father is an important spiritual rule. God has many reasons for telling you to honour your father. Fathers have done many things to save our lives that we are unaware of. They have sowed many good seeds in our lives and deserve to receive love, affection and honour. Absalom organised an army to attack his father's palace. He drove his father out of the palace and ran his father out of town. This behaviour of Absalom was to have serious consequences.

I once met a man who went by the name Absalom. I wondered how a person could be comfortable with such a name.

Over the years, I have experienced different sons attacking me. Some were very angry with me! Some rebuked me! Some shouted at me!

None of these sons have turned out well. Various woes befell their lives and ministries. The word of God cannot be broken. Honour thy father ...that it may be well with thee! Your ministry will come to an end when you have a bad relationship with your father.

I remember many churches that have had prominent pastors as fathers in the ministry. These fathers have been attacked by several sons they have raised up. Through the years, these senior pastors seemed to provoke their associate and assistant pastors until they became disloyal. Unfortunately, many of the assistant pastors became like Absalom and attacked their fathers. What happened to them? What happens to an Absalom? What happens to people who attack their fathers?

A curse is activated against all who attack their fathers. I want you to note the details of Isaiah's prophecy. It is a prophecy that protects God's servants.

Thou whom I have taken from the ends of the earth, and called thee from the chief men thereof, and said unto thee,

*The End of Absalom's Ministry*

THOU ART MY SERVANT; I have chosen thee, and not cast thee away. Fear thou not; for I am with thee: be not dismayed; for I am thy God: I will strengthen thee; yea, I will help thee; yea, I will uphold thee with the right hand of my righteousness.

Behold, all THEY THAT WERE INCENSED AGAINST THEE SHALL BE ASHAMED AND CONFOUNDED: THEY SHALL BE AS NOTHING; and they that strive with thee SHALL PERISH. THOU SHALT SEEK THEM, AND SHALT NOT FIND THEM, even them that contended with thee: THEY THAT WAR AGAINST THEE SHALL BE AS NOTHING, AND AS A THING OF NOUGHT.

Isaiah 41:9-12

***What happened to the rebels?*** They were ashamed: Over the years, all that were incensed against their fathers were ashamed and confounded. Many of them were ashamed that their predictions of the downfall of their father did not happen. Rather, the father continued to grow from grace to grace.

Many were shamed because they thought they could destroy their father's ministry with their words, their criticisms, their writings and their videos. Many Absaloms were soon identified by the masses as disgruntled, discontented failures. These Absalom characters were soon unravelled and their complaints were seen for what they really were.

It was a matter of time before everyone could see that they were men who simply did not want to accept correction. Their criticisms and negative words were soon seen as the death gargle of disenchanted and disappointed men.

***What happened to the rebels?*** They became as nothing, they became as a thing of nought: Many of these people became nothing in the ministry. They turn into nothing! Many of them go round begging for money. I have encountered several pastors who go round begging for money. Why should a minister of God turn into a beggar? Why should they go round from church member to church member asking them for gifts and begging them for hand-outs?

Perhaps, this is the most striking outcome of an Absalom and of someone who attacks God's servants. Nothingness! Notice how many times the scripture emphasizes the nothingness of those who are incensed against God's servants. They are condemned to become a thing of nought. They are condemned to become nothing.

***What happened to the rebels?*** Thou shall seek them and not find them: If you search through the city you cannot find these rebellious people. If you were to ask in the city for well-known pastors and thriving men of God, their names would never be mentioned.

Their churches never grew! The ministries they started became like day-old chicks that never grew to the size expected. These day-old chicks ate all the food that was given to them but could only grow into tiny, little muscular chickens. Whenever a committee of pastors in the city is being formed, their names never come up as potential members.

You cannot even find them when you are looking for them. The fate of an Absalom is indeed a catastrophe!

***What happened to the rebels?*** They perished: Many who attack their fathers are destroyed. Absalom was destroyed because he attacked King David whom God had anointed to sit on the throne. David's sin with Bathsheba was not sufficient to disqualify him from sitting on the throne. The throne belonged to the one who was anointed to be there. It is only God who gives a throne to the king. Absalom had no right to climb up onto the throne of Israel.

That is exactly what Lucifer attempted to do when Lucifer said, "I will ascend!" Anyone who is trying to ascend without God lifting him up is destroying himself. To perish is to be destroyed. Some of these people ended up dead! Some ended up burnt to death! Some had their families destroyed! Some had their businesses and jobs terminated! Some had their churches dissolved! Some became sick! Some had their children becoming rebellious! They that strive with thee shall perish! The outcome of an Absalom is not good!

# CHAPTER 9

# The End of Gehazi's Ministry

But Gehazi, the servant of Elisha the man of God, said, Behold, my master hath spared Naaman this Syrian, in not receiving at his hands that which he brought: but, as the Lord liveth, I will run after him, and take somewhat of him. So Gehazi followed after Naaman. And when Naaman saw him running after him, he lighted down from the chariot to meet him, and said, Is all well? And he said, All is well.

My master hath sent me, saying, Behold, even now there be come to me from mount Ephraim two young men of the sons of the prophets: give them, I pray thee, a talent of silver, and two changes of garments. And Naaman said, Be content, take two talents. And he urged him, and bound two talents of silver in two bags, with two changes of garments, and laid them upon two of his servants; and they bare them before him. And when he came to the tower, he took them from their hand, and bestowed them in the house: and he let the men go, and they departed. But he went in, and stood before his master.

And Elisha said unto him, Whence comest thou, Gehazi? And he said, Thy servant went no whither. And he said unto him, Went not mine heart with thee, when the man turned again from his chariot to meet thee? IS IT A TIME TO RECEIVE MONEY, AND TO RECEIVE GARMENTS, AND OLIVEYARDS, AND VINEYARDS, AND SHEEP, AND OXEN, AND MENSERVANTS, AND MAIDSERVANTS? The leprosy therefore of Naaman shall cleave unto thee, and unto thy seed for ever. And he went out from his presence a leper as white as snow.

**2 Kings 5:20-27**

# Covetousness Will End Your Ministry

**Let your conversation be without covetousness; and be content with such things as ye have: for he hath said, I will never leave thee, nor forsake thee.**

**Hebrews 13:5**

Covetousness is when a person desires something wrongfully. It is important not to have wrongful desires. When you are covetous you wish for things eagerly but wrongly. Gehazi was desirous of money and clothing. He was desirous of prosperity in a wrong way. He longed for silver, gold and other goodies that were not meant for him.

Encountering Naaman at close quarters stirred up his cravings for money and wealth. He could sense the wealth and prosperity of Naaman and he wanted some for himself. Be careful when you encounter wealthy people. Do not let their wealth and success stir up inordinate and inappropriate desires in you. Wealth is attractive. It is easy to fall in love with the trappings of success and wealth. You must not allow encounters with rich people to change your orientation and vision for life.

Gehazi was destroyed by his encounter with Naaman. He imagined getting all the things that Naaman had. He now also wanted to receive money, and to receive garments, and olive yards, and vineyards, and sheep, and oxen, and menservants, and maidservants! These new desires that grew in Gehazi led him to destroy himself and his ministry.

Gehazi's ministry was brought to an end by covetousness. Your ministry will come to an end if you give yourself to covetousness! It is so obvious when you listen to certain people preaching that they are after money and wealth. It is obvious when you watch certain people travelling around, that they are being driven by their desire or need for money.

Look around and you will see how many ministries are brought to an end because of a love for money. All the ministries that are filled with a strong desire for money and wealth have brought an end to their real effectiveness in the gospel. Look closely and you will see that even though certain pastors and prophets may have flashy cars and houses, they have little impact as far as the preaching of the gospel in the world is concerned.

Over the years, I have watched several men of God ministering the word of God. Over the years, I have also noticed a clear change in the impact of their ministries. Usually, the first half of their ministries was dedicated to preaching the basics and the foundations of Christ. The second half of their ministries emphasized a lot of fundraising, taking offerings and encouraging of people to give their money. Over the years, if you were spiritual enough, you would sense the change in the level of the anointing as the desire for more and more money grows.

A desire is an important thing. God punished Eve with a desire for a man! A desire can lead you to your punishment and to your curse. You must be careful of the desires you allow to lurk within you.

It is important to be filled with a desire for God. It is important to be filled with a desire for ministry. It is important to be filled with a desire for the anointing. The desire you have within you for the ministry will lead you into the ministry. It will lead you to your destiny in God.

Gehazi did not inherit the anointing. He could have had a double portion of God's anointing as he walked with Elisha. But he was a deceptive character looking for money. There are many deceptive characters in the church of God. They claim to be servants of God but they are actually servants of their own bellies. Gehazi is a warning to all ministers of the gospel. Desire the anointing and you will live! Seek after the Holy Spirit and you will do well!

From now onwards, look out for covetousness! Do not let evil desires develop within you. Do not let wicked desires lead you to your curse. Do not let any desires for other things bring an end to your ministry. Keep desiring God! Keep desiring the anointing! Keep desiring revelation!

# CHAPTER 10

# The End of Vashti

> If it please the king, let there go a royal commandment from him, and let it be written among the laws of the Persians and the Medes, that it be not altered, That Vashti come no more before king Ahasuerus; and let the king give her royal estate unto another that is better than she.
>
> Esther 1:19

*The End of Vashti*

# Pride and a Sense of Entitlement Will End Your Ministry

Vashti is the perfect example of someone who became too used to the privilege of being a queen. Her ministry was to help her husband. Her divine call was to be at the right hand of her spouse. But she became too big for that role. She lost focus! She refused to come when she was called. Your life and ministry will come to an end when you become too big for your shoes. When you can no longer be commanded, when you can no longer be sent, when you can no longer be called upon at any time, you are too big for the ministry.

Many pastors' wives have lost their place as the true helpers of their husbands. It is natural for an assistant to grow in pride and a sense of entitlement. This attitude leads to aloofness and detachment. Many pastors' wives have become unwilling partners, not impressed with their husbands any longer.

Many ministers' wives are just like Vashti. They are unyielding and opinionated. They love to take photographs and pose as ideal wives but it is all a cover-up. The beautiful outward presentation is all fake. It is a compensation for the wickedness and the spirit of Vashti. What a big controversy is created when pastors commit fornication or adultery! Yet, the origin of most fornication and adultery is found in Vashti-like wives who are inflexible, unpleasant, cold and unemotional about loving their pastor-husbands.

One day, a Christian husband said to his counsellor, "I have not had sex with my wife since we had a baby one and a half years ago. She has many reasons for not having sex."

He remarked cynically, "I know how to be an unbeliever! I have had many girlfriends in the past."

What do you think that meant?

He continued, "I have told her this is the last time I am having this discussion about sex with her." He was determined to go outside his marriage and find a willing, exciting and jovial friend who would be excited about sharing his bed with him. Of course, when he did, he was accused of fornication and adultery but he did not mind at all.

It is sad when women become too big for their role as wives. That is the spirit of Vashti. They become icy and callous. These strict "housekeepers" and "school mistresses" are not pleasant partners. Is it a wonder that these struggling husbands would seek joviality, jollity and jocundity outside their marriages?

When you express joviality, it means you are endowed with a hearty joyous humour. When you express jollity it means you are in good spirits and in a festive mood.

When you express jocundity it means you are being cheerful, merry and gay.

Dear wife, please learn your lessons well and maintain your position. The end of Vashti came when she was too big for joviality, jollity and jocundity.

Dear pastor, remember that pride will end your ministry. Pride will cause you to have nowhere to preach. Proud people are always discarded. Many proud men are too big for real ministry. It is sad that many people are too big for ministry. They are too big to go to the lowly cities, towns and villages that are teeming with souls. Many ministers only travel to the great and famous cities in America and Europe for ministry. But there are vast lands in many nations that need the gospel even more.

People need the Lord! Are we now too big for real ministry? Are we too big to go to the towns and villages preaching about the Lord? Are you too big for real ministry? Do you need to have a hotel and a big honorarium in order to preach the word of God? What are your requirements for preaching the gospel? Are you also going to charge a lot money for preaching? Are you also going to present an invoice and expect people to pay thousands of dollars before you do the work of ministry?

# CHAPTER 11

# The End of a Congregation

And Jehu said, Proclaim a solemn assembly for Baal. And they proclaimed it. And Jehu sent through all Israel: and ALL THE WORSHIPPERS OF BAAL CAME, so that there was not a man left that came not. And they came into the house of Baal; and THE HOUSE OF BAAL WAS FULL FROM ONE END TO ANOTHER. And he said unto him that was over the vestry, Bring forth vestments for all the worshippers of Baal. And he brought them forth vestments. And Jehu went, and Jehonadab the son of Rechab, into the house of Baal, and said unto the worshippers of Baal, Search, and look that there be here with you none of the servants of the Lord, but the worshippers of Baal only. And when they went in to offer sacrifices and burnt offerings, Jehu appointed fourscore men without, and said, If any of the men whom I have brought into your hands escape, he that letteth him go, his life shall be for the life of him.
And it came to pass, as soon as he had made an end of offering the burnt offering, that Jehu said to the guard and to the captains, GO IN, AND SLAY THEM; LET NONE COME FORTH. AND THEY SMOTE THEM WITH THE EDGE OF THE SWORD; and the guard

and the captains cast them out, and went to the city of the house of Baal. And they brought forth the images out of the house of Baal, and burned them.

2 Kings 10:20-26

## Idolatry Will End Your Ministry

Jehu called as many people as possible to come and make a big sacrifice to the idol, Baal. This big sacrifice to Baal caused the end of that congregation. An entire congregation perished because they worshipped idols.

The story above reveals how an entire congregation can be wiped out.

The love of security, the love of money, the desire for wealth will wipe out your church. The new idols are a love for security, a love for family, a love for happiness, a love for a good life, a love for good children, a love for grandchildren, a love for a happy home and a love for peace. As people keep on preaching and imparting the desire for human success, peace and wealth, the church dies slowly.

Many years ago, the church did not have as much money as it has had in recent times. Yet, the church was more effective in winning the world to Jesus Christ. Gradually, the love for God and His work has been replaced with a love for security, a love for family, a love for happiness, a love for a good life, a love for good children, a love for grandchildren, a love for a happy home and a love for peace. Indeed, these things have become the new idols of the church and its members.

Your idol is what you give up everything for. Your idol is what you yield to and what you bow down to. Your idol will make you rise early and make a big sacrifice to it. Indeed, big sacrifices have been made to have security in life. Big sacrifices have been made to have a good family! Big sacrifices have been made to have happiness! Big sacrifices have been made to have a good life. Big sacrifices have been made to have good children! Big sacrifices have been made to have grandchildren! Big sacrifices have been made to have a happy home! Big sacrifices have been made to have peace!

Have big sacrifices been made for the church? Have big sacrifices been made for the gospel?

Have big sacrifices been made to win souls? Have big sacrifices been made to build churches? Have big sacrifices been made to go on missions? Have big sacrifices been made to enter nations and spread the word of God? Have big sacrifices been made to evangelize the world? Have big sacrifices been made to support missionaries? Your god is the one for whom you make the big sacrifices.

Today, many Christians worship the idol of money, peace, security and good living. This idol is presented to the church as that which must be sought after and that which must be attained. Your god is the one who can make you wake up early in the morning to work very hard. Your god is the one you sacrifice to. Your god is the one you give up everything for.

Idolatry has brought an end to real evangelism and worldwide missions. This trust in the idols of security and peace has brought about the end of evangelism in the world today. You can hardly find an evangelist anywhere in the world today. Some years ago, there were real American missionaries in almost every country of the world. You can hardly find missionaries out on the field today.

The end of the church comes when these idols of safety, success and wealth are glorified by pastors. Christians, under the guidance and inspiration of their pastors, will give up everything for money, peace, security and successful living. Few people are prepared to go into the world and give themselves up for the ministry because pastors do not encourage them to do so. Yet these same people are prepared to sacrifice their families and live apart for many years in order to achieve success in life.

The end has come to many parts of the church because of the curse of yielding to idols. As the church fails to sacrifice to God, it gradually diminishes.

Instead of sacrificing to God, the modern church is sacrificing to demons. The sacrifices which people make are actually being made to devils. Are you sacrificing to devils or are you sacrificing to God?

**But I say, that the things which the Gentiles sacrifice, THEY SACRIFICE TO DEVILS, and not to God: and I would not that ye should have fellowship with devils.**
**1 Corinthians 10:20**

# CHAPTER 12

# The End of Judas' Ministry

When the morning was come, all the chief priests and elders of the people took counsel against Jesus to put him to death: And when they had bound him, they led him away, and delivered him to Pontius Pilate the governor.

Then Judas, which had betrayed him, when he saw that he was condemned, repented himself, and brought again the thirty pieces of silver to the chief priests and elders, Saying, I have sinned in that I have betrayed the innocent blood. And they said, what is that to us? see thou to that. And HE CAST DOWN THE PIECES OF SILVER IN THE TEMPLE, AND DEPARTED, AND WENT AND HANGED HIMSELF.

Matthew 27:1-5

# Treachery Will End Your Ministry

Treachery, disloyalty, duplicity, deceitfulness and betrayal will bring an end to your ministry. The punishment for treason is always death.

The betrayal of Judas is remarkable because Judas managed to present himself as one of the most trusted and trustworthy people in Jesus' life. When someone presents himself as trustworthy and shockingly, is later found to be a very different person, it creates a stir and a crisis that is not easily wiped away.

Judas was not just a disloyal person. He was more than disloyal. His disloyalty was combined with a deep and long-standing deception that was difficult to see through. None of the disciples had the faintest inkling about Judas' activities. At the dinner table, they all wondered what Jesus was talking about when He spoke of being betrayed. What would the betrayal involve? The disciples truly wondered. Then came the shock that it was none other than their trusted treasurer who secretly had links with the enemy.

A Judas is someone who is secretly an enemy but poses as a high-level insider for as long as he can. In the secular world, when a traitor or a mole is discovered, he is quickly eliminated. The story of Eli Cohen, the Jewish spy who lived in Syria is the shocking example of how deeply an enemy can penetrate. Eli Cohen rose up so high within the Syrian society and was so trusted that he was about to be appointed as the Deputy Minister of Defence for Syria.

Imagine that! Having an enemy appointed as the Minister of Defence! When he was discovered, he was immediately hanged and his body displayed in the centre of Damascus. Traitors are usually not given a chance. Any explanation from such a highly trusted person simply does not hold any longer. Do away with all Judases! The end of Judas is execution!

There will, by all means, be a Judas in your ministry. If you have not yet seen one, remember that you will. If you are following the footsteps of Jesus and walking on the *Via Dolorosa* (the way of suffering and pain), you will see all the things that Jesus saw. One of the things that Jesus encountered at the end of His ministry was Judas Iscariot. Judas is the total experience of treachery, treason, unbelievable betrayal and deep-seated deception. It is possible that you may become a Judas one day. Make sure you are never involved in anything that betrays and shockingly deceives the one who has trusted you. If you are ever diagnosed as a Judas, you must know that your end is to be hanged, just as Judas was hanged. May all those who present themselves as Judas be hanged in the name of Jesus! Judas has the capacity to end a ministry.

One day, someone asked about the death of Kathryn Kuhlman. Why did she die? Someone who knew her very well said that Kathryn Kuhlman's heart was broken because of treachery, treason and betrayal. He said Kathryn Kuhlman was unable to handle the betrayal that she experienced at the hands of the people who worked with her.

One day I spoke to a great man of God who was at the end of his ministry. At a point in his ministry, his wife had left him. He had experienced many terrible things in the church. One day, a trusted worker with whom he had worked for many years also suddenly abandoned him. Although he had survived the trauma of divorce and other ministry catastrophes, the shocking departure of his trusted worker devastated him more than his past experiences. Indeed treachery is a difficult thing to experience and overcome. It can bring you to the end!

Disloyal people bring about the death of a church. Within three days, Judas had brought Jesus' ministry to an end. Do not forget what has been done for you! Don't pretend! Don't accuse! Don't let ignorance make you a Judas! Don't be a dangerous son!

Disloyalty is a very dangerous characteristic. It is something that must be dealt with urgently and decisively. I have written many books on this subject[1]. Someone listened to me preaching about disloyalty and wondered whether I was angry about something. Another person was concerned for my health when he heard me speaking about disloyalty. Another person listened to me speak about disloyalty and asked if there was a crisis going on somewhere.

Unfortunately, these people have no idea about the dangers of disloyalty. I once met with a pastor who had had a 3000-member congregation. He told me a sad story of how a disloyal person took away his members, leaving him with only eighteen people. These eighteen people included his wife and children. Indeed, his church came to an end because he left the church with a disloyal man.

All forms of disloyalty will end a church and a ministry. Treachery and treason definitely have the power to end a ministry. You must be fierce and resolute when you are dealing with disloyal people. You must not deal with the enemy in the spirit of benevolence.

---

[1] *See the Loyalty Series by Dag Heward-Mills; Parchment House*

## CHAPTER 13

# The End of the Church's Ministry

And unto the angel of the church in Sardis write; These things saith he that hath the seven Spirits of God, and the seven stars; I know thy works, that thou hast a name that thou livest, and art dead. BE WATCHFUL, AND STRENGTHEN THE THINGS WHICH REMAIN, THAT ARE READY TO DIE: for I have not found thy works perfect before God. Remember therefore how thou hast received and heard, and hold fast, and repent. If therefore thou shalt not watch, I will come on thee as a thief, and thou shalt not know what hour I will come upon thee.

Revelation 3:1-3

*The End of the Church's Ministry*

In the scripture above, we see how the church is ready to die or end. When a church is ready to die it means that the church is about to come to an end. You may not know that many churches started gloriously but are closed down today. Those churches have come to an end.

The will of God is that you bear fruit and that your fruit abide. When the church comes to an end, it means that your fruits have not prevailed. Jesus said, I will build my church and the gates of hell will not be able to close it down (Matthew 16:18). We must do whatever we can to build the church in such a way that it never comes to an end. That is the will of God for the church: a church that never ends!

God is speaking to you about His work. He wants to use you to build a church that remains till Jesus comes. A statement by Mendell Taylor struck my heart. He said, "The church must send or it will end." How true these words are. As soon as you stop sending, your church is ending. Your church begins to die when you stop sending people out. Your ministry begins to wither when you stop sending.

Jesus said, "Go ye into all the world and preach the gospel" (Mark 16:15). Jesus sent us into the world. After demonstrating His power and His greatness to His disciples, Jesus stood in the Holy Land and sent His disciples into the whole world. Did Jesus not want to build something great in Jerusalem? Jesus had said earlier that He would build the church. How can you build a church by sending people away? That is the wisdom of God. The church becomes stronger and greater when we send people away on missions. The church becomes weaker when we stop sending people out!

The church must become a missionary church again. Every church must send missionaries into the world. You must send missionaries into your community. You must send missionaries into your city. You must send missionaries into the whole nation. You must send missionaries into other nations. You must send missionaries to the ends of the world.

The church is a living body; so when a function is denied it, it becomes diseased! When you deny a church its function of moving and sending people, it begins to die. The body is meant to move around. When movement stops, disease and sickness set in.

And Jesus came and spake unto them, saying, All power is given unto me in heaven and in earth.

Go ye therefore, and teach all nations, baptizing them in the name of the Father, and of the Son, and of the Holy Ghost: Teaching them to observe all things whatsoever I have commanded you: and, lo, I am with you alway, even unto the end of the world. Amen.

Matthew 28:18-20

### The Early Church Did Not End

The early church did not end. The early church encountered the greatest form of persecution ever to be seen by any section of the church. The early church had no money, no financial power and no special privileges. Yet it went on and on and grew till it dominated the whole world.

**And with GREAT POWER gave the apostles witness of the resurrection of the Lord Jesus: and great grace was upon them all.**

**Acts 4:33**

It is time for us to copy what the early church did otherwise our ministries will come to an end.

1. **The church must send people to JERUSALEM.** Jerusalem speaks of the cities and communities where you live today. Let us send so that we do not end!

   But ye shall receive power, after that the Holy Ghost is come upon you: and ye shall be witnesses unto me both in

JERUSALEM, and in all Judaea, and in Samaria, and unto the uttermost part of the earth.

Acts 1:8

2. **The church must send people to JUDEA.** Judea speaks of the surrounding cities and the surrounding nations. Let us send people there so that we do not end!

But ye shall receive power, after that the Holy Ghost is come upon you: and ye shall be witnesses unto me both in Jerusalem, and in all JUDAEA, and in Samaria, and unto the uttermost part of the earth.

Acts 1:8

3. **The church must send people to SAMARIA.** Samaria speaks of nations with different kinds of people. These people are so different, with different languages, that it takes an even greater effort to send the gospel there. Let us send people there so that we do not end.

But ye shall receive power, after that the Holy Ghost is come upon you: and ye shall be witnesses unto me both in Jerusalem, and in all Judaea, and in SAMARIA, and unto the uttermost part of the earth.

Acts 1:8

4. **The church must send people to the uttermost parts of the earth.** The uttermost parts of the earth speak of the furthermost nations from where you are located. Let us send so that we do not end!

But ye shall receive power, after that the Holy Ghost is come upon you: and ye shall be witnesses unto me both in Jerusalem, and in all Judaea, and in Samaria, and unto the UTTERMOST PART OF THE EARTH.

Acts 1:8

# CHAPTER 14

# The End of Babylon

And after these things I saw another angel come down from heaven, having great power; and the earth was lightened with his glory. And he cried mightily with a strong voice, saying, BABYLON THE GREAT IS FALLEN, IS FALLEN, AND IS BECOME THE HABITATION OF DEVILS, AND THE HOLD OF EVERY FOUL SPIRIT, AND A CAGE OF EVERY UNCLEAN AND HATEFUL BIRD.
For all nations have drunk of the wine of the wrath of her fornication, and the kings of the earth have committed fornication with her, and the merchants of the earth are waxed rich through the abundance of her delicacies.

*Revelation 18:1-3*

## Fornication Will End Your Ministry

Fornication and adultery are a major reason why ministries are shut down and come to an end. Even when the fornication is not discovered, the end has begun. I remember a man of God who received several warnings from God to straighten out his life. He lived an ostensibly impeccable life and had a squeaky clean reputation of being a champion of good marriage and marital purity.

However, behind this façade of purity and holiness was a life of persistent sin. After years of successfully living in hidden sin, a vision was given to a prophet. In the dream this prophet saw a huge velvety cloth being pulled back and to the prophet's amazement, the man of God was under the velvety cloth with a woman. A voice said, "Your ministry is wiped away!"

The prophet did not understand the vision and thought to himself, "What stupid vision have I just experienced? Perhaps I have eaten too many hamburgers." But the prophet was wrong about the interpretation of his dream. Within three months of having the dream, the man of God was exposed and his deceptions were discovered. Indeed, the prophet's dream was an indication from the Lord that He was sending an angel of revelation to uncover and to end his ministry.

When I read the story of this encounter, I understood how this man of God had been exposed through a series of unusual circumstances. To the ordinary eye, it was just unfortunate circumstances that came together to expose the man of God. However, the vision of that prophet revealed that a supernatural power was at work to end the ministry of this deceptive priest. God sent His angel to interrupt the continued deception of that congregation.

Fornication is a principal doorway through which demons and evil spirits enter a minister's life. Demons are always looking for entry points to enter a minister's life. It is of great importance that you fight the tendency to commit fornication. Demons enter your life whether people know about your fornication or not. Do not deceive yourself into thinking that once things are hidden, they are okay. Demons are comfortable even if they are not seen. The presence of devils will gradually destroy the house in which the devils are.

The desire to commit fornication is in every man. Paul said, I keep under my body and bring it into subjection (1 Corinthians 9:27). What exactly was Paul fighting? Was he fighting demons? No! He was controlling and subjugating his flesh. It is sad that your whole Christian life will be plagued with these evil desires. I can understand why Jesus would only want to live for thirty-three years on this earth.

The scriptures above show how demons entered Babylon because of fornication. Your desire to keep demons out of your life should give you extra strength and motivation to fight fornication for the rest of your life. God is helping you to resist every form of demonic infiltration in your life. Do not think of fornication as an ordinary sin. It is an unusual sin that opens the doors to hell. Demons of all types fly into the soul of those who engage in this sin.

Demons enter your ministry whether people know about your fornication or not. Do not deceive yourself into thinking that once things are hidden, they are okay. Receive supernatural power, wisdom and understanding to combat all attempts to make you a secret fornicator, and to end your ministry!

Many marriages push the spouses towards fornication. Indeed, marriage may either help protect you from fornication or actually push you into it. You must be careful about the type of marriage you enter into. Marriage has a potential of taking you one step nearer the temptation to live in fornication and receive an influx of demonic powers into your life. If you have already entered a difficult marriage, you must trust God to show you how to survive the temptations that may be heightened by your marriage. Indeed, being married to a stiff, unemotional, cold and asexual woman can push you into fornication.

And the light of a candle shall shine no more at all in thee; and the voice of the bridegroom and of the bride shall be heard no more at all in thee: for thy merchants were the great men of the earth; for by thy sorceries were all nations deceived.

And in her was found the blood of prophets, and of saints, and of all that were slain upon the earth.

Revelation 18:23-24

Babylon the great fell through the demonic powers that flooded the city through fornication. Spiritual creatures, unclean and hateful birds flew into Babylon once the doors were open through a life of serial fornications. Fornication can end your ministry! Do everything to prevent it in your life.

# CHAPTER 15

# The End of the World

**And as he sat upon the mount of Olives, the disciples came unto him privately, saying, Tell us, when shall these things be? and what shall be the sign of thy coming, and of the end of the world?...**

**And this gospel of the kingdom shall be preached in all the world for a witness unto all nations; and then shall the end come.**

**Matthew 24:3, 14**

*The End of the World*

The world as we know it will be destroyed. The cities of the world will be destroyed.

But the day of the Lord will come as a thief in the night; in the which the heavens shall pass away with a great noise, and the elements shall melt with fervent heat, THE EARTH ALSO AND THE WORKS THAT ARE THEREIN SHALL BE BURNED UP. Seeing then that all these things shall be dissolved, what manner of persons ought ye to be in all holy conversation and godliness,

2 Peter 3:10-11

The nations of the world and the earth will pass away with a great noise and great heat. The world is already heating up. Temperatures are increasing every day. Everyone can feel the entropy in the world increasing. The wars and the terrorism in our world are increasing in spite of all the interventions of the United Nations. The tensions that we feel are just signs of the end.

So what is going to precipitate the end of the world? What will cause the end to come? *The preaching of the gospel of Jesus Christ to the ends of the earth is what will precipitate the end of the world.*

The arrival of the coronavirus brought an end to travel in the world. It brought an end to church services, soccer matches, shops, airlines and many businesses. Indeed, the pandemic was a token for evil to the world. But this is still not the end of the world.

The world will not be brought to an end by the nuclear weapons we have built. If the nuclear weapons that have been created are deployed on earth, it is estimated that three billion people will die on earth in one day. One small nuclear bomb could wipe out everything within three to eight kilometres from the place the bomb is detonated. Yet, unleashing this mighty power intentionally or unintentionally will not be a trigger for the end of this world. The end of the world will be precipitated by the preaching of the gospel to all nations.

**And this gospel of the kingdom shall be preached in all the world for a witness unto all nations; and then shall the end come.**

**Matthew 24:14**

The preaching of the gospel will not change the nations of the world, per se. The preaching of the gospel will be a witness against the world. The preaching of the gospel will bring about a cataclysmic conclusion to this world.

The preaching of the gospel will be used as evidence against the nations of the world. The world will be asked, "Do you remember my servants who came preaching over here?" There will be much evidence for the judgment of the nations of the world.

# CHAPTER 16

# The End of John the Baptist's Ministry

At that time Herod the tetrarch heard of the fame of Jesus, And said unto his servants, This is John the Baptist; he is risen from the dead; and therefore mighty works do shew forth themselves in him. For Herod had laid hold on John, and bound him, and put him in prison for Herodias' sake, his brother Philip's wife. For John said unto him, It is not lawful for thee to have her. And when he would have put him to death, he feared the multitude, because they counted him as a prophet.
But when Herod's birthday was kept, the daughter of Herodias danced before them, and pleased Herod. Whereupon he promised with an oath to give her whatsoever she would ask. And she, being before instructed of her mother, said, give me here John Baptist's head in a charger. And the king was sorry: nevertheless for the oath's sake, and them which sat with him at meat, he commanded it to be given her.
And he sent, and beheaded John in the prison. And his head was brought in a charger, and given to the damsel: and she brought it to her mother. And his disciples came, and took up the body, and buried it, and went and told Jesus.

                               Mathew14:1-12

# A Woman Can End Your Ministry

John the Baptist's ministry was ended by a woman. The end of your ministry can be caused by a woman. There are several ways in which a woman can bring an end to your ministry.

1. **A woman can end your ministry through her wickedness.**

   **I asked, "What is it?" He replied, "It is a basket." And he added, "This is the iniquity of the people throughout the land."**

   **Then the cover of lead was raised, AND THERE IN THE BASKET SAT A WOMAN!**

   **HE SAID, "THIS IS WICKEDNESS," and he pushed her back into the basket and pushed its lead cover down on it.**

   **Zechariah 5:6-8 (NIV)**

   The wickedness of a woman is usually revealed when she has power over her man. A woman has power over her man when she has sex with him. If a woman has sex with a man outside marriage, she gains power to destroy the man and his reputation. It is then that you see her wickedness fully manifested. When a woman has sex with her Christian husband in marriage, she also gains power over him because he needs her. He depends on her for his physiological and sexual needs. It is here that you also see the power and potential wickedness of the Christian woman. Many men are sent into adultery because of the unwillingness and wickedness of their wives.

2. **A woman can end your ministry through her influence.**

   **And when the woman saw that the tree was good for food, and that it was pleasant to the eyes, and a tree to be desired to make one wise, she took of the fruit thereof, and did eat, and gave also unto her husband with her; and he did eat.**

   **Genesis 3:6**

A woman's influence on her husband is mysterious, to say the least. Although she is not the head, she has great power to influence him.

"There be three things which are too wonderful for me, yea, four which I know not: The way of an eagle in the air; the way of a serpent upon a rock; the way of a ship in the midst of the sea; and the way of a man with a maid." (Proverbs 30:18-19)

Through emotions, tears, pleadings, crying, sexuality, sensuality and other forms of persuasion, a woman can sway the mind of a right-thinking man. It happened to Adam and it can happen to you. Adam's life and ministry came to an abrupt end after he listened to his wife's persuasive request. What pleas, cries and requests are you getting that are taking you from the will of God? Be careful that a woman does not end your ministry!

### 3. A woman can end your ministry through her fears and jealousies.

**For Herod had laid hold on John, and bound him, and put him in prison for Herodias' sake, his brother Philip's wife. For John said unto him, it is not lawful for thee to have her.**

**Matthew 14:3-4**

Herodias ended the ministry of John the Baptist. She had taken over someone's husband. Herodias was afraid of the challenge she was getting to her new position. Herodias did not feel secure as the wife of Herod. Herod was quite happy with her but Herodias did not feel secure because of the comment she had heard that John the Baptist had made. Many women are driven by their insecurities.

Perfect love casts out fear. Fear destroys your way of loving. Many of these women are empowered by the demon of fear and not by the Holy Spirit. You can imagine what it is like to encounter a woman who is demonically controlled by a demon of fear, When a minister is not strong enough to hold and maintain his course, these forces can bring an end to his ministry. I have seen pastors cower like timid children in the presence of their wives. They are unable to express themselves or do what they really want to do because of their wives.

# CHAPTER 17

# The End of Onan's Ministry

And Judah said unto Onan, Go in unto thy brother's wife, and marry her, and raise up seed to thy brother. AND ONAN KNEW THAT THE SEED SHOULD NOT BE HIS; AND IT CAME TO PASS, WHEN HE WENT IN UNTO HIS BROTHER'S WIFE, THAT HE SPILLED IT ON THE GROUND, LEST THAT HE SHOULD GIVE SEED TO HIS BROTHER. AND THE THING WHICH HE DID DISPLEASED THE LORD: wherefore he slew him also. Then said Judah to Tamar his daughter in law, Remain a widow at thy father's house, till Shelah my son be grown: for he said, Lest peradventure he die also, as his brethren did. And Tamar went and dwelt in her father's house. And in process of time the daughter of Shuah Judah's wife died; and Judah was comforted, and went up unto his sheepshearers to Timnath, he and his friend Hirah the Adullamite.

**Genesis 38:8-12**

# Throwing Your Seeds Away Can End Your Ministry

There are several ways in which you can waste the seeds that God has given you. Onan is an example of someone who threw away the seed God gave him. Throwing his seed to the side displeased God greatly. Today, many ministers are throwing away the seeds that God gave them. What does this mean?

**Now the parable is this: The seed is the word of God.**

**Luke 8:11**

There are many things that are seeds. A Word from God is a seed. A book is a seed. A message is a seed. A person can be a seed. A song is a seed. God gives us seeds and expects us to plant them.

Every time you throw seeds away, it displeases God. Seeds are miracles. No human can manufacture seeds. A seed is a self-generating, life-giving nugget that can create new life. What has God given you that can create new life? Are you using it wisely or are you throwing it away?

One day, I had a vision. In this vision, I saw myself walking towards an army. The army was clad in shining armour and the soldiers' weapons were gleaming in the sunshine. It was a very well prepared army. In the vision, I approached this army and I heard people shouting behind me, "Be careful. You will be shot. You are going to get yourself killed." But I kept walking. When I reached the frontline of the troops I put my hand in my outer pocket and took out some seeds. I threw the seeds at the front row of the soldiers.

When the seeds touched them, they were hit with such power that they all fell down. I was amazed at the power of these seeds. I kept throwing more and more seeds at the army and they kept tumbling down until the whole army was flat on the ground. I was amazed at the power of the seeds I had in my pocket. When I came out of this vision, God spoke to me. He told me, "I have given you seeds. These seeds are your most powerful weapons. Use them wisely and use them well." From that time, I developed a proper respect for the power of seeds. You must also develop a proper respect for the power of seeds. What seeds has God given you? The seed is the word of God! Your seeds are the words and teachings God has given you.

### 1. You throw away your seeds by rejecting the call of God.

The call of God is the word of God to you. God's Word calls you out from among men. God expects you to respond. To reject His seed and throw it away is to have gone the way of Onan and wasted the seed.

### 2. You throw away your seeds by not preaching the gospel.

When the gospel is not preached, the seed of salvation is wasted. Onan wasted the seed God had given him. Do not waste an opportunity to preach the gospel. Today, the church does not preach the gospel in its pure and simple form. We have all sorts of motivational and encouraging sermons that are close and parallel but very different from the real gospel.

### 3. You throw away your seeds by not teaching the Word.

God is not happy when you do not deliver the messages He has given you. God expects you to deliver the seeds He has given you in time. God expects you to deliver meat in season. God expects you to write certain books by a certain time. God expects you to teach certain things by a certain season.

> **Who then is a faithful and wise servant, whom his lord hath made ruler over his household, to give them meat in due season? Blessed is that servant, whom his lord when he cometh shall find so doing.**
>
> **Matthew 24:45-46**

### 4. You throw away your seeds by not investing in missions.

God expects every church to send young men out as missionaries. What is going to happen when you do not send your young men out into the world to preach the gospel? You will experience the wrath of God and you will be condemned to barrenness when you throw away your young missionaries. Have you not noticed how the church has shrunk because we have thrown our young men into business rather than into the ministry?

# CHAPTER 18

# The End of Isaac's Ministry

And it came to pass, that when Isaac was old, and his eyes were dim, so that he could not see, he called Esau his eldest son, and said unto him, My son: and he said unto him, Behold, here am I. And he said, BEHOLD NOW, I AM OLD, I KNOW NOT THE DAY OF MY DEATH: Now therefore take, I pray thee, thy weapons, thy quiver and thy bow, and go out to the field, and take me some venison;

Genesis 27:1-3

# Weariness Can End Your Ministry

The end of Isaac came when he was old, tired and weary. The end of your ministry can come when you are old, tired and weary. You must avoid becoming an old, weary pastor of your church. Many churches have died because they are pastored by old, weary warriors who have worked for God for many years but do not have younger replacements to take over from them. Notice that Isaac could not see well. His eyes were dim. This speaks of losing vision. In other words, Isaac had lost the energy and also lost the vision.

As I travelled around, I noticed how most churches had elderly, tired-looking men as pastors. When I preached at pastors' conferences, I noticed how bored these elderly people looked when I was preaching. I also noticed how easy it was for them to fall asleep whilst I was preaching. You can't blame them! They were tired! They were weary! And they were way past the age when they should have stepped aside. It is important to give opportunities to younger people. Younger people can take up the ministry if you give them the opportunity.

I visited a pastor who had a vibrant growing church. He would tell me how many people got saved every night. He was very zealous about soul winning. He always strove to build something bigger and better for God. I noticed, as he got older, that he stopped talking about church growth and his conversations gradually changed. He was not backsliding in any way. He was simply getting older and weary of the job. Indeed, he never handed over the practical work of ministry to his successor.

Some years ago I found out that there was something called a coadjutor bishop. A Coadjutor is a bishop who assists another bishop with the right of succession. I found this an interesting concept. The concept of installing a bishop whose role is basically waiting for the opportunity to take over the ministry is an amazing preparation for the future. There is always a need to prepare for our older years and a creeping weariness and tiredness. Most ministers do not accept that they are older and not as sharp as they used to be. The church will end when weary people are not replaced with brighter, sharper and younger talents.

# CHAPTER 19

# The End of Ahab

And they continued three years without war between Syria and Israel. And it came to pass in the third year, that Jehoshaphat the king of Judah came down to the king of Israel. And the king of Israel said unto his servants, Know ye that Ramoth in Gilead is ours, and we be still, and take it not out of the hand of the king of Syria?

And he said unto Jehoshaphat, Wilt thou go with me to battle to Ramothgilead? And Jehoshaphat said to the king of Israel, I am as thou art, my people as thy people, my horses as thy horses. And Jehoshaphat said unto the king of Israel, Enquire, I pray thee, at the word of the LORD to day.

THEN THE KING OF ISRAEL GATHERED THE PROPHETS TOGETHER, ABOUT FOUR HUNDRED MEN, AND SAID UNTO THEM, SHALL I GO AGAINST RAMOTHGILEAD TO BATTLE, OR SHALL I FORBEAR? AND THEY SAID, GO UP; FOR THE LORD SHALL DELIVER IT INTO THE HAND OF THE KING.

And Jehoshaphat said, Is there not here a prophet of the LORD besides, that we might enquire of him? And the king of Israel said unto Jehoshaphat, There is yet one man, Micaiah the son of Imlah, by whom we may enquire of the LORD: but I hate him; for he doth not prophesy good concerning me, but evil. And Jehoshaphat said, Let not the king say so. Then the king of Israel called an officer, and said, Hasten hither Micaiah the son of Imlah. And the king of Israel and Jehoshaphat the king of Judah sat each on his throne, having put on their robes, in a void place in the entrance of the gate of Samaria; and all the prophets prophesied before them. And Zedekiah the son of Chenaanah made him horns of iron: and he said, Thus saith the LORD, with these shalt thou push the Syrians, until thou have consumed them. And all the prophets prophesied so, saying, go up to Ramothgilead, and prosper: for the LORD shall deliver it into the king's hand.

1 Kings 22:1-12

# A Multitude of False Preachers and Prophets Can End Your Ministry

Ahab was a king of Israel. He survived many crises, including the tragedy of being married to Jezebel. How did his reign end? He was brought to the end of his life and ministry by four hundred false prophets who lied to him. These prophets were more popular than the true prophets.

Today, many people's ministries are coming to a conclusion because of a myriad of popular false teachings. Teaching about money, wealth and success is a good thing. I believe in it. However, over-emphasizing it creates a false message with a spirit of greed and selfishness. This false message imparts worldliness, imparts earthly-mindedness and imparts a grasping mentality to the church.

Today, churches are full of worldly Christians who just want all that the world has to offer. "Give me the world! Give me all that the world has! I want more money! I want to be safe from all possible dangers! I want security! I want long life! I want many cars! I want to live in a western country!"

Yes, you will have safety! You will have prosperity! You will have a good life! God is love! God is happy! God likes everything you are doing! God loves you! God wants you to be rich!

This message is nice! Unfortunately, this message is preached by many false prophets. This message of safety is encouraged by many false preachers who have over-emphasized earthly things.

The end can come to your life and ministry when you want to be accepted by the masses. The end can come to your ministry when you want to be popular. The end can come to your ministry when you want everyone to like you. Micaiah was the only one who warned Ahab that he would die in that battle. All the other four hundred prophets gave a sweet-sounding victory message to the king. Unfortunately the king believed this sweet-sounding message.

Today, many are giving sweet-sounding messages to all and sundry: Everyone is going to be happy! Everything is going to be okay! Everyone will have his own car! But many of these prophecies do not come to pass. Notice how the false prophecies were completely set aside and proved wrong by the death of Ahab. Four hundred prophets were wrong and only the lonely voice of Micaiah was right.

> And a certain man drew a bow at a venture, and smote the king of Israel between the joints of the harness: wherefore he said unto the driver of his chariot, Turn thine hand, and carry me out of the host; for I am wounded. And the battle increased that day: and the king was stayed up in his chariot against the Syrians, and died at even: and the blood ran out of the wound into the midst of the chariot. And there went a proclamation throughout the host about the going down of the sun, saying, Every man to his city, and every man to his own country. So the king died, and was brought to Samaria; and they buried the king in Samaria.
>
> 1 Kings 22:34-37

Ahab could have listened to Micaiah. Unfortunately, Micaiah was a lonely and unpopular voice. God has a lonely voice that He wants you to listen to.

"And Micaiah said, If thou return at all in peace, the LORD hath not spoken by me. And he said, Hearken, O people, every one of you." (1 Kings 22:28)

God will lead you to the right books and teachings of those who are truly speaking the word of God today. Pray about it. Do not be put off because of the lonely voice of Micaiah. It may save your life.

Your ministry will end when you accept the multitude of false and deceptive preaching that misleads you into living a life of ease on this earth whilst forsaking the work of ministry.

# CHAPTER 20

# The End of Ministry

For rebellion is as [serious as] the sin of divination (fortune-telling), And DISOBEDIENCE is as [serious as] false religion and idolatry. Because you have rejected the word of the Lord, He also has rejected you as king.

1 Samuel 15:23 (AMP)

DISOBEDIENCE is as bad as the sin of sorcery. Pride is as bad as the sin of worshiping idols. You have rejected the Lord's command. Now he rejects you as king.

1 Samuel 15:23 (NCV)

# Disobedience Can End Your Ministry

Disobedience can end your ministry. Almost every bad thing that can happen in the ministry starts with disobedience. I always remember a teaching by Derek Prince. He said God spoke to him when He called him. God told him that in the ministry "You must learn to obey Me in the big things and the small things". There is no area in life and ministry where disobedience to God is acceptable.

Disobedience brings your ministry to an end. You must do whatever God tells you to do. Obey God when you read the Bible. Obey God when He speaks to you by His Spirit. Obey God when he speaks to you through others. Obey God when He speaks to you through preaching. Whatever you do, make sure you obey God.

# Ten People Whose Ministries Ended Because of Disobedience

### 1. Disobedience ended Adam's ministry.

And unto Adam he said, Because thou hast hearkened unto the voice of thy wife, and hast eaten of the tree, of which I COMMANDED THEE, SAYING, THOU SHALT NOT EAT OF IT: cursed is the ground for thy sake; in sorrow shalt thou eat of it all the days of thy life; Thorns also and thistles shall it bring forth to thee; and thou shalt eat the herb of the field; In the sweat of thy face shalt thou eat bread, till thou return unto the ground; for out of it wast thou taken: for dust thou art, and unto dust shalt thou return.

Genesis 3:17-19

### 2. Disobedience ended Saul's ministry.

BECAUSE THOU OBEYEDST NOT THE VOICE OF THE LORD, nor executedst his fierce wrath upon Amalek, therefore hath the LORD done this thing unto thee this day.

1 Samuel 28:18

3. **Disobedience ended the ministry of the sons of Eli.**

   If one man sin against another, the judge shall judge him: but if a man sin against the LORD, who shall intreat for him? Notwithstanding THEY HEARKENED NOT UNTO THE VOICE OF THEIR FATHER, because the LORD would slay them.

   1 Samuel 2:25

4. **Disobedience ended the ministry of Solomon.**

   And the LORD was angry with Solomon, because his heart was turned from the LORD God of Israel, which had appeared unto him twice, And had commanded him concerning this thing, that he should not go after other gods: but he kept not that which the LORD commanded. Wherefore the LORD said unto Solomon, Forasmuch as this is done of thee, and THOU HAST NOT KEPT MY COVENANT and my statutes, which I have commanded thee, I will surely rend the kingdom from thee, and will give it to thy servant.

   1 Kings 11:9-11

5. **Disobedience ended the ministry of the priests, Nadab and Abihu.**

   And Nadab and Abihu, the sons of Aaron, took either of them his censer, and put fire therein, and put incense thereon, and offered strange fire before the LORD, WHICH HE COMMANDED THEM NOT. And there went out fire from the LORD, and devoured them, and they died before the LORD.

   Leviticus 10:1-2

6. **Disobedience destroyed Israel.**

   And an angel of the LORD came up from Gilgal to Bochim, and said, I made you to go up out of Egypt, and have brought you unto the land which I sware unto your fathers; and I said, I will never break my covenant with you. And ye shall make no league with the inhabitants of this land; ye shall throw down their altars: but YE HAVE NOT OBEYED MY VOICE: why have ye done this?

Judges 2:1-2

### 7. Disobedience brought about the death of the neighbour.

And a certain man of the sons of the prophets said unto his neighbour in the word of the Lord, Smite me, I pray thee. And the man refused to smite him. Then said he unto him, BECAUSE THOU HAST NOT OBEYED THE VOICE OF THE LORD, behold, as soon as thou art departed from me, a lion shall slay thee. And as soon as he was departed from him, a lion found him, and slew him.

1 Kings 20:35-36

### 8. Disobedience caused children to mourn.

Hear me now therefore, O YE CHILDREN, and depart not from the words of my mouth. Remove thy way far from her, and come not nigh the door of her house: Lest thou give thine honour unto others, and thy years unto the cruel: Lest strangers be filled with thy wealth; and thy labours be in the house of a stranger; AND THOU MOURN AT THE LAST, when thy flesh and thy body are consumed, And say, How have I hated instruction, and my heart despised reproof; And HAVE NOT OBEYED THE VOICE OF MY TEACHERS, nor inclined mine ear to them that instructed me!

Proverbs 5:7-13

### 9. Disobedience caused pastors to be eaten up.

Go up to Lebanon, and cry; and lift up thy voice in Bashan, and cry from the passages: for all thy lovers are destroyed.

I spake unto thee in thy prosperity; but thou saidst, I will not hear. This hath been thy manner from thy youth, THAT THOU OBEYEDST NOT MY VOICE. THE WIND SHALL EAT UP ALL THY PASTORS, and thy lovers shall go into captivity: surely then shalt thou be ashamed and confounded for all thy wickedness.

Jeremiah 22:21-22

## 10. Disobedience brought about the end of fathers.

BUT THEY AND OUR FATHERS DEALT PROUDLY, AND HARDENED THEIR NECKS, AND HEARKENED NOT TO THY COMMANDMENTS, AND REFUSED TO OBEY, neither were mindful of thy wonders that thou didst among them; but hardened their necks, and in their rebellion appointed a captain to return to their bondage: but thou art a God ready to pardon, gracious and merciful, slow to anger, and of great kindness, and forsookest them not.

Nehemiah 9:16-17

## 11. Disobedience brought about the end of the Israelites in the wilderness.

For the children of Israel walked forty years in the wilderness, till all the people that were men of war, which came out of Egypt, were consumed, BECAUSE THEY OBEYED NOT THE VOICE OF THE LORD: unto whom the LORD sware that he would not shew them the land, which the LORD sware unto their fathers that he would give us, a land that floweth with milk and honey.

Joshua 5:6

## Conclusion

Through this little book, many ministry endings have been shown to you. We have seen the way ministry can be brought to an end in this book.

To the making of many books there is no end! Be encouraged with these few words!